BABY BOOMERS
FACE GRIEF—

Survival and Recovery

JANE GALBRAITH

• Canada • UK • Ireland • USA •

Note for Librarians: A cataloguing record for this book is available from Library and Archives
Canada at www.collectionscanada.ca/amicus/index-e.html

Order this book online at www.trafford.com
or email orders@trafford.com

Most Trafford titles are also available at major online book retailers.

© Copyright 2009 Jane Galbraith.
All rights reserved. No part of this publication may be reproduced, stored in a retrieval
system, or transmitted, in any form or by any means, electronic, mechanical, photocopying,
recording, or otherwise, without the written prior permission of the author.

Printed in the United States of America.

ISBN: 978-1-4120-7424-7 (sc)
ISBN: 978-1-4122-0405-7 (e)

 www.trafford.com

North America & international
toll-free: 1 888 232 4444 (USA & Canada)
phone: 250 383 6864 ♦ fax: 812 355 4082

This book is dedicated to my Mother who gave me unconditional love all of my life.

It is also dedicated to all those who have or will face the loss of a parent and will survive.

ACKNOWLEDGEMENTS

This book was written with the love, support and encouragement of many people in my life who believed the subject of grief was important.

There have been many roadblocks to having this book published and without the ongoing encouragement and faith from my friends I don't know if it would have happened. I want to thank all of my friends for their never-ending cheerleading of this project. There are too many people that fall into this category to name them all but you know who you are!!!

It saddens me that my love and partner, Bruce Kilmer, did not come into my life until after my mother's death. My mother would have certainly loved him. From the moment I mentioned the idea of this book he has been totally supportive of the idea and anything I had to do to make it a reality. He is the one that picked up my spirits when I lost faith or confidence at times. I am grateful I am going through life with him by my side.

I need to take this opportunity to thank my best friend

Barb Dudley who was kind enough to allow me to share the poem she wrote for me after my mother died. Her poem captured so well her understanding of my pain and the relationship my mother and I shared. Barb's writing ability has always been amazing and her unrelenting support has been there unconditionally from the start and has been so very appreciated through the years.

I need to also thank John Duff, my childhood friend, for his assistance in creating the cover of the book, which reflected the difficulties one encounters with grief but also the hope symbolized by the eagle, that through this process your life can become a richer and fuller one.

Lastly, I am very grateful for the feedback that I have received from those that I have shared this book with prior to its publication. Many of these people have been friends of friends and their feedback and stories have been very appreciated and helpful as I put the finishing touches on the book. Some of their comments have been included. If those that read this book felt validated in their varying grief reactions then I have accomplished what I intended with this book.

Foreword

Individuals facing bereavement differ in many significant ways. However, they often have in common the experience of isolation and of being unable to measure the "normalcy" of their loss. As a counselor it is important to be able to recommend a book that deals with the process of grief as a personal experience and which offers non-judgmental ways of measuring its impact on us.

Framed in the context of the "boomer" generation Jane starts with her own open discussion of the death of her mother, but extends her discussion to all aspects of loss. She describes how death affects the individual, his or her relationships, as well as how societal attitudes can worsen the impact of loss on us all. She gives specific ideas about the preparation before the impact of loss and the suggestions for constructively dealing with the aftermath of death.

From the outset, she notes that many of us find unexpected change to be difficult. Her book provides a careful antidote to the tendencies in our culture to avoid facing grief and to the "quick fixing" of personal loss.

Throughout, the theme is that of not judging one's reactions; of not trying "to do grief according to the book"; to stay open to the possibility that grief can eventually create change. Her book is open, practical and ultimately conveys a strong and positive message to anyone struggling with loss.

In the past I have feared recommending books about loss, as they can in spite of their intent, leave people feeling worse. This book will leave people feeling confirmed in their experience and hopeful for their future.

Dennis Walker
September 2005

REVIEWS AND COMMENTS

Dr. Dan Dalton, Ph.D., C. Psych.

Jane Galbraith's book on Grief should be required reading for all middle aged children. For most of us born during the 50s and 60s coping with the inevitable loss of our parents will occur over the next two decades. By taking us through her own personal journey in a very sensitive and insightful manner, Jane gives to all Baby Boomers an opportunity to share in each other's loss and to benefit from each other's courage. Writing in a style that is engaging and easy to read, Jane maintains a beautiful balance that carries one through feelings of emotional despair while maintaining an objective and reality based attitude.

By the end of the book the reader is left with a solid understanding of the grieving process and a sound appreciation of how the deep pain experienced by the loss of ones parents can also serve to powerfully enrich and ennoble ones life.

Dr. Sue Loper, Library Director
90 Million baby boomers will, in the next 20 years, face the loss of one or both parents through death or disease. This book discusses society's lack of acceptance of grief in general and the way past generations have taught us to deal with this life event. In this writer's opinion this generation, known as the baby boomers, through the sheer force of their numbers, has the ability to make positive changes in the way this and succeeding generations handle grief. The grieving process is explained; how it differs for all of us; that there is no "right" way to grieve and that the pain of grieving cannot be avoided. Suggestions are offered for managing grief. Ceremonies and rituals surround death and grieving is discussed and suggestions about how to structure a meaningful ceremony to honour loved ones are given. The book makes it clear that change can occur in our society, with this generation, that will allow people to manage grief in a constructive way; that sharing experience can allow others to be more prepared and more open in dealing with this life altering experience and that people can find comfort in knowing that others have had similar experiences. This book allows a glimpse into what we will all face and some strategies to cope with our loss, in an easy to read, personal narrative format.

Chris Armstrong

The content is so timely and relevant for all of us to react and reflect on. For me the messages are clear. Dealing with grief is a process that cannot be avoided. It is time for us to identify, understand and act on our inability to openly and comfortably express our emotions and feelings.

Anne Low

This book provided me such comfort after I lost my mom at a young age. Jane's personal story touched my heart and it provided me with comfort through such a difficult time. It was so refreshing to read a book on loss that wasn't theoretical. This book is "human" and that's just what you need when you can't stop questioning why you are feeling the way that you are. It reconfirms that nothing is wrong with you and that others have been through a similar battle.

CHAPTERS

There are times in our lives that change us and we are not prepared. My mother's death was one of those times. I thought I would know how I would react, but I was greatly mistaken. I could not have predicted the intense emotion that I felt or the change in my perspective of life.

After several years of living in a world without my mother, I realized that my generation, the baby boomers, would soon be ambushed by the surprises I experienced. I have learned that our society does not "do" grief well, but I believe that the baby boomers' experiences with grief could positively impact the way this area of human suffering is viewed. It will take, however, the sharing of experiences to make changes to our societal norms.

Knowledge about what to expect is often the first step in assisting someone to cope. We all have life experiences to share with each other. We just need to start talking about a subject that has never been an easy one to discuss. We no longer have to maintain the wall of silence erected by previous generations.

Some issues are addressed more than once in this book, as they are associated with many different aspects of the topic.

I wish that no one had to go through this experience, but I know they will and the sharing of experiences will aid them in this process. Together we can make it better for ourselves and generations to follow.

The following poem expresses how to get through the grief process with a deeper understanding of our lives.

As You Journey Through All Seasons

As you journey through all the seasons of your grieving,
You will discover what countless others have discovered
before you:
That you have changed.
You will never again be the person you once were.
You will have lost,
But in addition to the losing–because of the losing–
You will have gained.
You will be yourself, and you will be more
than yourself.
Some people describe this process as transformation.
Others call it resurrection.
Whatever words you choose,
The result is the same.
Something new will have come to life.
Something unexpected will have been born.

Reprinted by permission from WINTER GRIEF, SUMMER GRACE
by James E. Miller, copyright © 1995 Augsburg Fortress.

WHY WRITE NOW?

Death is inevitable. Death is always premature no matter how old you are. Everyone knows that it will happen to them and to the people they love most in the world. Parents often come to mind first, as we usually survive our parents. This is often the first significant experience we have with death. Even though it may be an event that we can foresee, it takes a greater toll on us than we could ever anticipate or imagine.

Also unexpected, is the change people go through as a result of a loved one's death. Too bad there's not a school where you could enroll to get through one of the most difficult experiences of your life. If there were, it would mean that we were talking about this subject and that people experiencing the same reactions would be listen-

5

ing, sharing and helping others through this life transition.

A death is the trigger for a powerful emotional rollercoaster ride. It is a life-altering event that will stop you in your tracks and is not talked about enough in our society. This is particularly true after the funeral when things have returned to so-called "normal". You would gladly give your seat up on this ride, which could not be classed as an amusement ride. There is nothing amusing about it. Since most of us will have this experience, I want to warn you about a period in your life that will happen no matter what you do or don't do to prepare.

What I have been talking about is GRIEF. Since it is not appreciated, valued or given the respect it deserves in our society, it is difficult to engage people in conversation about the subject. Unfortunately, however, it has the potential to be a life-altering emotion that can result in very positive or very destructive consequences. It has been talked about and written about by many professionals, but go into any big bookstore and compare the section on death, dying and bereavement to that on weight loss, how to find your soulmate or many other self-help subjects and you will see what our society values. The magnitude of grief in our lives and how it subsequently affects everyone around you is not easily seen. It becomes a well-hidden burden shortly after the funeral. Grief has become "off limits" as an acceptable subject of conversation in our society.

Grief is one of the next life stages baby boomers will be facing together. By their numbers alone, they have had a tremendous effect on society in many ways. How could the ninety million of this generation in North America not continue to influence our culture?

There has never been a time in history that business has had such a distinct market to target any number of products. All research for new product development first looks at the baby boomers to see what they need now and in the future.

Sometimes being part of such a large group is comforting, as there will be many others to talk to about similar life situations. You relate to people the same age with similar life experiences, who understand you. Look at all the magazine articles targeted to this age group. I feel sorry for our parents or the generation Xer's who must be sick of reading about the trials and tribulations of the baby boomers. Our parents are saying, "Been there, done that!" and the Xer's are saying, "Who cares about us?"

Every boomer life event is analyzed and reported on. Boomers have become information connoisseurs. Having grown up in the information age, they crave and receive information about everything and anything. This generation has been the impetus for the self-help era and their desire for knowledge is insatiable.

This generation will be going through the most difficult time in their lives – together! We are approaching the age where losing people we love, that have always been in our lives, will become a reality and a tragedy. Our major loss will be the death of our parents, but grief can occur when we lose anything significant. Although there is comfort in numbers, many baby boomers will not be prepared for this event. Simply put, we don't understand grief or its effect on our lives.

It is not difficult to understand why we would not be prepared for the wave of grief that we will collectively face at relatively the same time. Look at how our parents faced these situations in the past. Most were brought up with the stiff upper lip mentality; it would not be socially acceptable to "break down" while going through this life event. We have always heard that people were "holding up" or "being strong" under the strain of a funeral. We may have already experienced a grandparent's death, and you would have taken the cues from your parents as to how to face this unfamiliar life experience. My guess is that all was seemingly back to "normal" shortly after the funeral service. Most likely, a wall of silence was erected at this time. Is this how you'd want your children to react to your death?

I would like to be optimistic and think we'll all learn from and support each other during this time. Moreover, that certainly could happen. Knowing about the effects of grief and mourning on your emotional and physical health, however, I am concerned that "we" won't have the internal resources to help ourselves, let alone anyone else.

A wonderful consequence of this would be our generation breaking through the culture's taboos of grieving, changing the way our society handles grief.

Our present culture does not allow us the freedom to grieve in a healthy way. Grief is a difficult topic to discuss. It is "in the closet" for lack of a better term. For all our emphasis on communication, we still don't do well in this area. We are still probably concerned about being able to competently handle anything that comes our way. There must be a quick fix to get back to normal, we think. This type of thinking could lead to destructive behavior. Misdirected anger is just one example of a behavior that can disastrously affect many kinds of relationships. Ask any counselor who has seen unresolved grief come out in the strangest places. I am concerned that all this emotion of the baby boomers will end up creating life experiences we'd prefer not to live through.

With so many baby boomers going through this at the same time, my hope is more attention will be paid to grieving and bereavement, and finally it will get the understanding it deserves. That would be the proverbial silver lining to the cloud of grief that is hanging over this generation.

I want to say now that I wouldn't be considered an expert in the field of grief but I feel passionately about the subject. I have experienced the death of both parents, which showed me incredibly different emotions about the same life event. I have also learned a great deal from my nursing education, from my contacts through work with palliative care, bereavement professionals and facilitating bereavement groups. So, I have gained a certain perspective on this issue. Understanding grief has become very important to me.

Everyone has to go through this life experience alone and their journey will be as individual as they are. I will share my own experience with you, as best I can remember. It is shared as an example and not to say this is the way to grieve or you will experience everything I did. It is shared to give you some sense of the depth of feelings that might be experienced. My hope is we will have more compassion for our friends when they find themselves overwhelmed. Our society, the baby boomers in particular, can begin to set a better example for the next generation.

Many times the sharing of a personal experience can

help others going through a similar circumstance. It serves to validate unspoken emotions that others are feeling and unwilling to verbalize. Maybe my experience will help people feel they can cope with grief in their lives. I hope that eventually they will realize they have survived and this life experience has eventually had a positive effect on their lives.

I have had two parents die and the grief experience was very different. I can only describe what I felt during that period of my life. The difference in experiences was confusing. My mother's death significantly impacted my life, as we were extremely close and totally involved in each other's life. My father conversely had not been involved in my life to any great degree and his death did not have the same impact. It was several years after my mother's death, the first and most painful time that I sought answers to my questions about grief and its enormous affect on my life.

There is no preparation for the shock, loss of control, emptiness, and bewilderment you will feel when initially faced with this event. The most practical and organized baby boomer will not know what train just knocked them off their feet. Moreover, the feeling is frightening. After being an adult, totally in control of your life, you change when hit hard with grief and mourning. Like me, you probably have no idea of how hard you will be hit with this tidal wave of emotion when a significant loved one dies.

Many people think they know how they will react when someone extremely close to them dies. We underestimate the sadness, despair and often what feels like insanity that we will have to endure along the road to healing. I thought I knew how the sadness and grief would feel. I was shocked to find I had drastically underestimated its impact. It would have helped to talk with someone who'd had the same experience. Someone open and honest, who could tell me how they managed this major life event.

Through this time, we can learn many things that might have otherwise taken years to discover. You may start to question areas of your life that you had taken for granted up until now. These life lessons can only bring about a more positive experience, one that allows you to grow as a person. However, you must feel the pain, learn from the experience, and then share your perspective with others.

Without a doubt, this is a journey that we all have to take at one point. Each one is different and unique and has it's own distinct route to follow. However, it has no particular time frame and will vary from one person and experience to another. It will probably be much longer than you think.

This passage in life is inescapable. The event that plummeted you into your grief also changed your life forever. Your healing will eventually teach you how to live in the new world that was created when the loss occurred. You are now living in a world that is forever changed.

Although this inescapable journey may be unbearably painful, the outcome may find you a better and more compassionate person. Don't be afraid of the road you will take. You can take all the detours you want, but eventually the path will lead you to healing and coming to terms with your loss.

One way to get through less scarred is to use the resources that are close at hand—your friends and family. This crucial support is at your immediate disposal.

Talking to my friends, I realized that they were totally unaware of what they too would face someday. It took me some time to realize the impact this grief would have on the largest of generations in history and over a relatively short time frame.

This book developed in my mind as I realized that my generation was to be confronted with this colossal wave of grief. I had lived through grief and survived. At the same time, my life was irreversibly changed. I was wrong when I thought I would be prepared for the feelings involved with this life event. Others will be taken off guard when they have this experience, as I was. I felt an obligation to share the information I have learned. Most of the knowledge gained came from my own life experience. My nursing education and life experience could never have prepared me for this event even though I truly thought it would.

My hope is people will find this book beneficial. If reading it encourages people to be more open themselves and empathetic with their friends, it will be a success for me. Our culture does not allow us to deal with grief openly. I feel that our generation has the potential to change how our culture deals with grief.

Baby boomers have an opportunity to turn the effects of grief into positive outcomes. Grief needs to be dealt with when it comes. If not, it will turn up when you least expect it. If we learn how to help ourselves and those we care about, we can change the cultural norms and add richness to our lives that we wouldn't have had otherwise.

Everyone will be helped through this process with different activities. You must realize you are dealing with significant pain. There is value to experiencing pain, depression, anxiety, loss of control and bewilderment. You need to get through these passages to allow hope back into your life. And you will.

It scares me that all these baby boomers are entering this stage in their life totally unprepared for the onslaught of emotions they will be facing. It is important that we help ourselves as well as others through this complex time in our lives.

Nevertheless, there is light at the end of the tunnel. Looking back, it is worth all the effort it requires to get to a better place on the other side of the pain.

Friends and family will help you through this time. Other resources are available. Many are internal that you may not realize that you possess. Don't be afraid to use anything you think will console you to get through this difficult life passage.

The pain you experience when remembering your loved one will eventually turn to warm memories when you think about them and their life with you. The world will not be the same without them, but you will be different and hopefully better. You will always have them in your heart.

CHAPTER ONE

PERSONAL EXPERIENCE

On December 6, 1992, my mother went to bed and never got up again. We'd celebrated my birthday the day before and she was complaining of a cough and not feeling well. She stopped by the medical clinic to have her chest examined as a precaution and they had simply suggested a humidifier in the bedroom. This was the day my mother stopped participating in the world.

It was hard to believe that Mom couldn't do anything anymore. She'd always been active and vital. She enjoyed life and was involved in many activities. She was 71 years old. She probably wouldn't mind my telling her age now!

My mother was very involved with her friends, volunteer work, and especially me! Her intense interest in every aspect of my life was annoying for an independent adult. I now realise that having someone so interested in your life is a blessing and not a curse. Our contact was frequent and our lives were very entwined despite my attempts to live an independent existence. The fact was my mother played an extremely important and vital part of my life.

From the time Mom went to bed, she was tired to a point of exhaustion that I can't comprehend to this day, even finding it taxing to eat. Mom no longer had the strength to watch her favorite TV shows. Reading magazines or talking on the phone was also difficult. Our phone calls used to be quite long but not anymore.

I was desperate to get Mom to eat. I was hoping to keep up her limited strength and hopefully get some back. Tempting Mom with favorite foods was never successful. I felt very helpless as well as confused as to what was happening medically. I was not alone. The doctor despite all of the medical tests in the home had no conclusive results.

We kept thinking the illness was a virus and she had all the time in the world to recover. Living close would allow me to help her in the recovery phase while she was rebuilding her strength. This process would take a great deal of time and patience. The idea she may not recover was not in either of our minds. For many weeks, we kept trying to think of all the possibilities causing these symptoms. I asked many other health professionals I worked with for their opinion and there weren't many decisive conclusions.

One good part was how much time we had to talk. I was able to share some difficulties that I was going through in my life at the time. As always, she was very supportive whenever I had a life crisis. Despite not listening to her advice on occasion, I really did listen when the subject was more important. I did respect her advice although I didn't always take it. That was usually the time that Mom would have been justified in saying, "I told you so". Her display of restraint in this area was admirable. I don't know if I could have been so gracious.

One issue did nag at me the loudest throughout this time. Her fatigue was the most often voiced complaint. To use the word exhaustion, although close, did not adequately describe how tired Mom felt. It seemed as if she had been de-boned. She could barely sit at the kitchen table to eat. Talking on the phone, watching TV or reading even for a short time was too much for her. I felt she was rude to her dearest friends, and I'm sure they didn't understand. To me, this was frightening.

Medical knowledge is not always helpful, but information can assist you with the denial process. You can rationalize a severe illness into one less severe but with

similar symptoms. Thoughts about the profound tiredness Mom was feeling, were nagging at me I was trying
not to think about the possible long-term consequences.

By Christmas, Mom could no longer stay at home,
even with my help. She just wouldn't accept any assistance, except from me of course! Although home care
was the area of health care in which I was employed she
would have nothing to do with the idea. Yes, Mom was
a difficult patient.

Mom was getting weaker by the day from the tiredness
and from three weeks of scant food intake. We needed
some answers. Mom was afraid to be in her apartment,
except when I was with her. She never expressed that fear
until she was safely in her hospital room. I was the only
one she would allow to visit her in the hospital.

This uncertainty was bound to end. And it did. It was
like a bad dream when I heard the news. My mother's
doctor called and said, "Are you sitting down?" I immediately knew the news was not good. The doctor said the
results of the abdominal ultrasound showed metastatic
tumors in my mother's liver. They weren't sure where the
primary cancer had started. I was shaken to the core. I
felt like the floor had disappeared underneath me. It is
difficult to put into words.

My mother had not been informed of the news yet.

I told him that I wanted to be there when she was told. We agreed to meet in the doctor's lounge and then talk with Mom together. When we met, he told me there was another less serious possibility. This was the only ray of hope in this nightmare. At least this possibility had a treatment available. I knew what a diagnosis of liver metastases meant.

The doctor and I walked up to Mom's room. It was the longest walk I've ever taken. I was flooded with emotions, but wanted to be strong for the woman who'd always been so strong for me.

The doctor told her the news with empathy and compassion. I was extremely impressed with his delivery of this news. If I ever have to hear bad news, I want him to tell me. I remember my mother's eyes opening wide when she heard that this could be cancer. This was the only physical manifestation of any emotion she may have felt during the whole conversation. I was desperately trying to hold myself together. I had to be there for my mother whatever this situation would bring us.

She was very stoic and told me that she would have to fight hard. She wanted to be there for me, as she knew that I was about to end my marriage. She was thinking only of me even in the face of this devastating news.

My mother has always been optimistic and a fighter. She always saw the glass half full. She was also a great fatalist. We had been given the possibility of bad news, but also a ray of hope. That was all Mom needed to hear to hang on to for dear life.

There were more tests needed to determine which of the two diagnoses would be the right one and Mom wanted to find out as soon as possible. The test was a liver biopsy, which is not a pleasant experience. She didn't complain. She was different however when she returned from the biopsy. Mom was forgetting very basic information and that development scared me enormously. She was also somewhat weaker on one side than the other and required the assistance of two nurses to go to the washroom.

I knew my time with my mother was limited and I wanted to make the most of it. I thought of everything that I wanted her to know that I had never told her. I vowed to make the most of whatever time we had left in the loving, caring atmosphere that had always characterized our relationship. Sure, we had our share of knock-down, drag-out fights but we could never stay mad for long. One would always call the other and this was not considered surrender. I'm sure that my incredible need for independence contributed to many of the fights.

I found myself reviewing our life together and picking out the memories to remember together. There were many things I had not shared with my mother but felt she should know.

I had not reconciled myself to the idea that she would no longer be with me. The idea was truly inconceivable to me. This would be a time that denial was a valuable ally.

All of this occurred in a matter of two days, if that. Mom learned the news on Monday and then on the Wednesday, she experienced the slight weakness. It was during these days that I focused on my need to share my memories and thoughts with her.

On Thursday afternoon, I received a call from the palliative care nurse saying that Mom had suffered a stroke and had asked for me. I needed to get to the hospital quickly. When I arrived ten minutes later, my mother could not make any understandable sounds. I think she could understand me and seemed to react physically to my words, but I'll never know for sure. It was unbearable for me to know that my mother wanted to tell me something, but could no longer communicate. Never in my life have I felt so helpless.

That night Mom was in pain. They finally were able to control both her pain and agitation. The situation was now one I could no longer deny, even though I gave it my best shot. It was hard to deny when I had to call friends and family with the news.

When my mother slipped into a coma early Friday morning, the doctor said it would only be a short time. At that point, they knew she had liver metastases. It upset him that my mother and I had lost the ability to communicate due to the stroke. He was quite empathetic. He acknowledged this was a devastating loss for us.

When confronted with the obvious your thinking is affected in strange ways. It was difficult to come to grips with the reality of her death. I could still go to the hospital, feel her warm skin, talk to her and believe that she could understand. She was still alive!

All activities in my life stopped. Knowing Mom's condition and ensuring she was receiving the best care possible was my focus now. When not at the hospital, the waiting was intolerable. Every time the phone rang, I'd freeze. Was this "the" call? I recognized that I'd be facing the future alone without her guidance, support, and unconditional love that had always been there for me.

The emotions I went through at this time were incredible and exhausting at the same time. My mind was racing in a thousand different directions but without focus. I could not achieve any control over the thoughts, fears, and confusion I was feeling. It was a totally helpless and hollow feeling.

The waiting felt like a year, even though it was only a couple of days. Finally, the phone call came. Mom was close to the end and if I wanted to, I should come to the hospital. There was a snowstorm that night and the nurse was very concerned about the road conditions.

As I was dressing, the phone rang again. The doctor told me that Mom was gone. He asked if I still wished to go to the hospital. My last memories of her were not pleasant, but I did remember her warm skin against my face and didn't want other memories to replace those.

I returned to bed, feeling very alone in the world now. This feeling totally took me by surprise. As an independent woman, the feeling of aloneness shocked me. I felt I'd been set adrift in the ocean with no help or direction. It would take some time to get this flood of emotions under control.

Shock and grief swept over me with such intensity, I completely lost my sense of equilibrium. The physical pain caused by these emotions also surprised me. These emotions would not be experienced all at once. They came in an assortment of groupings and in waves. Just when I thought I was coping I would be hit by another wave of different emotions. The constant battering wore me down. This was a new experience for me and I wouldn't want to repeat it.

The initial shock of the news does not last too long. It almost distracts you from the reality of the situation. My experience with two deaths brought very different reactions. My first experience, my mother's illness and death, was short in duration and the most intense. My father's death came within six weeks of learning his diagnosis. It seemed eerily familiar as I managed my father's care. I didn't feel the same intensity of emotions as I did with my mother.

My reaction to my father's death was different, as was our relationship. My most active emotion was guilt because I wasn't feeling more emotion for my father. I was also focussed on the sense of loss for the end of any possibility of changing the relationship we had to one that was richer and fuller.

These two experiences show that the relationship you had with the deceased often dictates the degree of grief and mourning you will experience. No matter how intense the grief is, it needs to be addressed as part of our healing.

Looking back now I realize the process of grief changed my life in many ways. Life, as I knew it, was over but it also became richer as I explored a more spiritual existence. The priorities I had were replaced with others that offered so much more fulfillment. I am grateful for the love and support of my friends who understood and loved me as I made my way through this unknown journey.

CHAPTER TWO

GRIEF

Grief is your feelings and thoughts after you have lost someone special. Mourning is the outward expression of grief. People often are not able to display either grief or mourning to the world. This inability occurs for a variety of reasons.

This doesn't relate only to the loss of a loved one. Any significant loss such as divorce or loss of a job can create the same feelings and life passages as a death. No matter what the loss, grief is the result. Often a new loss triggers the pain of a previous loss not dealt with completely.

Our society puts limitations on how long it will take someone to grieve a loved one's death. You hear people say to the bereaved," Well, it's been a year now," or "Don't make any decisions for the first six months". That may not be bad advice, but it does not mean that the grieving process will be over in that time.

Grief is pain and unfortunately cannot be avoided by anyone. Many believe grief can be handled. This will only delay the unresolved pain that will eventually surface. You need to embrace the pain wholeheartedly. The role of hurt in this process is undervalued. Sayings like "Time heals all wounds", "God won't give you more than you can handle", and "You are holding up well" encourage the myth that the pain is short-lived. These clichés are not helpful and minimize the very real pain and loss felt at this time. These unrealistic expectations may encourage the bereaved to shut themselves away.

Grief and mourning are both needed for the healing of our souls. Destructive outcomes result when people do not deal with the grief they encounter in their lives. There is no predetermined time frame for the process to be complete. It is actually a continuous process going through many changes and stages of intensity. It is never really over.

Baby boomers need to have some idea of what to expect. There is no road map to follow. The road may become bumpy on this trip. There is comfort knowing where potential danger areas may be.

Elisabeth Kubler-Ross has written extensively on the stages of grief. She has written for both health-related fields as well as the public. She was one of the first to identify specific stages of grief and what to expect. She was a pioneer in this field.

I read a lot on the subject when I was going through this myself. Through that reading and my own experience, I have formed my own thoughts on grief and mourning.

Without a doubt, many stages and emotions are felt during this process. Anger, denial, shock, bargaining, acceptance, confusion, disorientation, sadness, guilt, blame, and depression are some that are experienced in no particular order. When different stages of grief will be felt is unique to each individual. There is no formula that applies to everyone or to every situation. It is also not necessary to travel through all of the stages. Stages may be skipped completely and others may take longer, depending on the individual.

Anyone experiencing grief should be aware of this and not try to stick to any formula that is suggested in any book. Your journey will not be predictable. If you expect to be through a certain phase by a certain time, you will just add more stress. You will already be overstressed physically and emotionally. Being aware of potential stages however is a good idea. They sneak up on you unexpectedly. You need to be aware of the possibility you will be subjected to them. Allow yourself to deal with each one as they come. There is no secret formula to follow. It doesn't exist. Don't hide or deny your emotions. You and only you can set the pace for your journey. The grief process cannot be rushed. Give yourself the time.

There may never be another time that you experience such a concentration of emotions. It completely takes you by surprise. I had no idea of the magnitude of the shock, hurt, aloneness and sadness I would face. You feel completely drenched in each emotion you experience. Most people don't realize the amount of energy it requires to grieve.

Intense and powerful emotions were not my only revelation. I was totally taken off guard by the way; these emotions would erupt unexpectedly to shake me to the core. They would not come on regular intervals, gradually increasing or decreasing in their intensity. Waves would bombard me with their varying force. It would take all I had to maintain my equilibrium and at times I thought, my sanity. Eventually you get as accustomed as anyone can to not knowing what is coming next. You have a heightened awareness the possibility exists at any time. Instinctively you feel like you're walking in a minefield and you'll never know when the next one will explode. The confidence you had in the past may have temporarily disappeared. Remember, there is no predictability or order to this onslaught of emotional surges.

People will have experienced deep and powerful emotions at other times in their life so this may sound familiar. The difference to me was that previously these feelings were experienced one at a time.

I felt emotions that I'd never encountered before, like complete disorientation and disorganization. Since I pride myself on my organizational skills, this was extremely disconcerting. I found it difficult to make decisions and when I did, to remember them. A numbness that felt like a filmy cloth draped over me. Nothing seemed as clear as it once did. Life appeared to be moving in different directions and it was unclear which direction to take. My sense of security in the predictability of life had evaporated. This was all new and scary for me.

You are confused so it's not easy for others to understand what you are feeling. Your behavior may have changed. It becomes difficult for you to explain it.

Physical symptoms may also take you off guard. Even someone in peak physical condition is not immune. What's often disconcerting is you are dealing with both the physical and emotional symptoms. In other words, you don't get a break!

Physical pain can manifest itself in a number of ways. An ache, tightness in the throat or chest or a pain in the stomach or chest is not uncommon. People could suspect they were having a heart attack. Emergency room records often indicate these pains as a physical reaction to an emotional state.

Your sleep patterns may also be disturbed. Whether it's difficulty getting to sleep or staying asleep, there are remedies available that will be discussed later. My greatest difficulty was falling asleep. Any disturbance to sleep patterns can have a significant impact on your emotional state.

Eating may pose another difficulty. People often lose their appetite when under stress. I lost ten pounds during this time. Many more pounds can be lost. When you are not eating correctly, you won't have the energy to deal with the many issues confronting you. On the other hand, others may eat more under the stress that grief causes. Weight gain has its own medical issues and problems.

There are many physical symptoms or concurrent symptoms that you may experience. Other symptoms could be anxiety, dizziness, nausea, and trembling. This is a difficult time when you no longer feel in control of your mind or body. Grief assaults every aspect of your person. There is no escape from injury in some way.

Every loss you experience will also be different. As you change so will your reactions. Any previous life experience will have an affect on how you deal with future stresses and grief. Everyone develops their own style of coping with painful experiences.

The relationships you have with different people affect your reaction to the loss. The depth of your attachment to the deceased, the history you share with the person, how much the person influenced and was a part of your life, your last experience with the deceased, your past experience with grief and how much support you have around you are all factors. There is a definite correlation with the depth of our feelings and our subsequent grief. The degree to which you grieve will express the degree to which you have loved someone.

Another factor to consider is whether this death is expected or completely unprepared for. Being caught off guard by an unexpected death brings many feelings into play in a much shorter time. When you are prepared for a loved one's death the grief may start earlier. The feelings at the time of death will often be the same.

When there is no longer a person to visit, no matter what condition they are in, this closes a door that can never be reopened. This finality often has the same depth of emotion attached to it whether the death is expected or not.

Many feel guilt, and I would suggest that this is a universal emotion. There is often a sense of relief that the deceased is out of their pain. Even though this is a sincere thought, it often triggers a sense of guilt that you could be so relieved. This is also true with survivors' guilt when several people have experienced a tragic event and only a few remain alive. Why have they lived when others died? The tragedy of September 11, 2001 would certainly be an example of these feelings experienced by those who were able to escape from such a nightmare.

What wasn't said or done before your loved one died can be a source of guilt. It is all the "what ifs" of what could have been done to comfort the person or perhaps to improve your relationship.

The quality of your last interaction can either be a comfort or produce immense guilt. Especially if the meeting involved an exchange of harsh words. Deal with guilt quickly. It can be very destructive, doesn't assist you during the grieving period, and requires a great deal of energy. Be kind to yourself and forgive yourself anything that may be creating this guilt. Try not to beat yourself up. Your loved one has already forgiven you.

Constantly, in the forefront of our minds are thoughts of the deceased. These are difficult to escape and they drain the energy and disturb the concentration you require to function in your daily activities. Everything seems to elicit thoughts of the loved one. Smells, sights and sounds are incredibly powerful in this regard. I found smells to be especially comforting. When at my mother's apartment I would often bury my face in her closet to remember her familiar perfume and was comforted by the feel of her clothes on my skin.

Feeling alone in the world is common no matter how much support you may have. Your world is no longer the same without the person that has always been in your life. You may feel unsociable and withdraw to heal. There is a tendency for people to shut down and close out the world. It may be done subtlety but as a friend, you should watch for it. It is quite different than feeling lonely. Aloneness has a depth to it. It is a very personal "you against the world" feeling. It may cause anxiety, since you don't know how to "fix" the situation. I felt it immediately when my mother passed away. It was a prominent feeling I experienced regularly. I'm sure for me being an only child was a factor. However, this feeling is not unique to only children. Even as an adult with siblings, you can feel orphaned when a parent dies. Many friends, with and without siblings, have shared with me that they have experienced similar feelings.

The flood of emotions and physical symptoms are confusing. It is not possible to prepare. If you are aware of what may come, it may be less upsetting. This is a normal part of the process no matter to what degree you are experiencing them.

Your confusion will no doubt leave you feeling that

everything is different. You may become tentative in your decision-making and life choices. At this stage, you probably shouldn't make any, since your reasoning may not be up to par. The uncertainty you feel is disconcerting and difficult to understand. The frustration felt can make you irritable or angry with everyone. You may feel that you are teetering on the edge of insanity. It takes time to make sense of this.

Your goal-setting ability may be impaired to some degree during this time. I'm not talking about life goals; even the daily errands that need to be done may prove difficult. There is often an inability to focus or concentrate on any task. Planning future activities is not possible for many at this stage.

You may feel like you don't know how to be happy anymore. It seems ludicrous, but you often don't remember what it feels like to be happy. If you do have a moment of joy there can be instantaneous guilt. You can't win. Despite the potential guilt, don't avoid the laughter. Its benefits are amazing.

The world is a different place. Everything that was taken for granted—like picking up the phone and hearing their voice or having someone to listen and encourage us is now gone. How you imagined you world in the future has changed. The person who once helped define who you were is no longer there to offer guidance. This will affect the rest of your life. This is not something you get over; rather it's a situation you learn to live with. You will develop an understanding of what this loss means to you.

The grieving process can change your values. You may look inward and reevaluate who you are, what you are, and where you are going. Every experience will feel differently than before.

Priorities get examined more closely now. Your priorities may seem out of kilter as you look at what you value. What seemed important yesterday may not seem so significant today. A small, touching scene with your children, friends, or pets may replace what used to be important to you. Now spending quality time with people who are important to you may seem much more valuable than wasting time on "things". You realize that the people you love most, you often take for granted. You start to look at your life with a new set of eyes and reevaluate what is truly giving you pleasure and what really doesn't matter.

Work often loses some of its importance. Not to say that your career isn't as important as other critical aspects of your life, but it's importance may change when other aspects of life are revisited. You may find yourself more focused on the quality aspects of both your personal life and your chosen career.

Many people look closely at their life choices; this exercise is often productive and can change your life direction for the better. It can be one of many positive effects of the grief process.

You will proceed through this process at your own pace and time. Each of us will have a distinct reaction to grief and how we try to adapt to our new world.

Don't let others try to tell you what you should or shouldn't do at this time. Even though it is a confusing time, you need to get through this in a way that is best for you.

Special days will often be difficult, but the first one is usually the worst. They magnify the absence of your loved one. Fear and trepidation are connected to special days such as birthdays, anniversaries, Mother's Day, Father's Day, Christmas, and the anniversary of their passing. You fear these events will take you back to the same emotional state when the event first took place. The focus of your thoughts will be centered around your loved one on those special days. However, the anticipation leading up to the day is often worse than the day itself. You may be filled with dread in the weeks before the day. Your imagination is often much worse than reality.

As each year passes, these days will gradually start to bring out warmer thoughts and feelings with less pain. You will find that remembering these thoughts actually feels good. Then you know that you are on your way to integrating this loss into your present world in a constructive way. This is an important part of the healing process.

I think the first anniversary of the death is the most dreaded and especially difficult to bear. You are often not far along in the grief process (no matter what you have read) to glide through this anniversary without excavating some major emotions.

I started reliving the last year's events about a month before the anniversary. In my case that is when the course of events started. It may start earlier in the year when there has been a drawn out illness. The anticipation of these events is often harder to bear than the actual day. You start second guessing what happened and how you could have changed the outcome. Human nature takes over at times.

The intensity of the pain changes as time passes. You can only sustain such pain for so long. You can start looking at photographs and remembering situations with love and laughter. There is hope the future will bring more good memories, even without our loved one with us.

Photos are a great way to encourage those memories. They make us feel closer to the person. I recall looking everywhere for pictures and chastised myself for not taking more snapshots when my mother was alive. She always wanted a picture, so I was grateful for all the shots she insisted that we take of the two of us. They are now my most treasured possessions.

Many of the loved one's possessions may become important to the bereaved, but none as much as letters, pictures, notes and mementoes. To hold a letter in your hand that the person you so loved had written can help bring back many reassuring memories. Inanimate objects such as a special chair can have the same emotional effect. You will be surprised at what will affect you.

I found a note after my mother died. We hadn't been able to talk and say goodbye so finding this note was like finding buried treasure. It now means more to me than anything I possess. The day I started the arduous task of sorting through her belongings the note appeared. I found it at the time I needed it the most. I was dreading the task I had before me and had set aside four days to get started on the long process. The note had been written five years before. I never knew of its existence. The note was with cards and letters my stepfather and I had given my mother over the years. I could hear her voice as I read it. It was a special gift from her to help me through my grief. It is now framed and in my house where I can read it often.

This is her letter:

Sun. Mar. 29th

My dearest Janie —

This afternoon I read over all these cards — the ones from Allister and from you — and you know it made me feel really loved. I will treasure them all for always. It reminded me what a loving caring wonderful daughter you have been and what a great husband I had in Allister.

Don't ever change — keep that marvelous ability to express your feelings — and one day I know that someone will open up his heart to you too the way Allister did so eloquently in these cards to me.

You are dearer to me than words can ever say and I appreciate so much all these lovely thoughts that you have put into words so beautifully for

Your mom.

41

Grief never will follow a straight path. You can tell you are starting to recover from the depths of grief when your every thought is not focused in the past. You come to know that you can re-build your life without that person in it and still be happy and fulfilled. Eventually you will have more good days than bad. There is always the possibility that a wave will hit you when you least expect it. They can't be avoided and can continue to happen for years. You will learn to deal with those waves and know that they will come less frequently and with less intensity as time goes by.

Some people can be quite embarrassed when these emotions suddenly take them by surprise. It is nothing to be embarrassed about and simply demonstrates the strong bond or connection you have had with someone you loved.

You can reap great benefits from such a hard won process. You may find your spiritual side. You may find that your priorities don't feel right anymore. This process reconstructs your life, as you knew it. The way you choose to live your life now can be the best tribute to your loved one.

CHAPTER THREE

THE CULTURE WE LIVE IN

Does the term "stiff upper lip" sound familiar to you? In our North American culture, it is how we get through difficult times. We were brought up to show strength in times of adversity and not to outwardly show our despair, sadness, and sorrow.

Many examples show us how to deal with these situations. Jacqueline Kennedy kept it all together throughout the funeral of her husband John F. Kennedy. She was held up as a shining example of courage in the most challenging situation. Even John F. Kennnedy Jr., only 3 at the time, will always be remembered for his stoic salute as his father's casket passed by him. In a way, you can understand them not showing their feelings openly, as they were so much in the public eye. They have however, served as an example that people tend to emulate.

Our culture does not do grief well! This is an understatement in my opinion. Our present culture does not allow us the freedom or permission to grieve. Grief is a difficult topic to discuss. For all our emphasis on communication, we still don't do well in this area. Mourners don't have to wail to show their grief. The issue is the atmosphere in our culture that a mourner faces when they show a display of grief. We don't feel safe to grieve openly in our culture. There are times that this becomes less accepted. The result is many people are walking around carrying the pain of grief on their shoulders. I guess I would call them the "walking wounded".

As baby boomers are hit with this wave of grief, we need permission to express our grief in a healing way. Right now, our society does not readily grant us this privilege.

I hope we will show more empathy and compassion when so many will go through this experience at the same time. Doing this will assist ourselves, our friends, spouses, family and our children to react to grief in a new and different way. We have the opportunity to change a cultural norm.

There is a widespread ideology that discussing and

openly expressing our feelings would be a sign of weakness and would be embarrassing, especially for men.

It is too bad that fear and shame often keep us from sharing our feelings. When emotions are expressed, it allows the other person to understand what you are experiencing and offer their sympathy. A deeper understanding could help each other be more supportive when we need it. We will all need it eventually.

Coping has been the buzzword for the baby boomers. We have been conditioned to think that coping is how we need to live. Certainly, it is good to cope with what life throws us.

"How to" and "self help" books fill the bookstores. Why would we need to talk to someone and share our feelings if a book can solve our problems? Books are great resources, but only one of many resources available to you.

More baby boomers will be seeking out professional help. The professionals available help tremendously to sort out our feelings. Seeing a professional either is seen as a "cool" thing to do or a sign of weakness. In actuality, many of the counselors will tell you that they don't often have patients asking for help with their grief. However, it frequently becomes apparent that a current loss in their life has brought to the surface an unresolved grief from their past. Losing our parents may trigger a past grief that has not been dealt with. This may magnify our loss. Counselors say unresolved grief can surface in many unexpected ways.

If our grief is not dealt with, the baby boomers will create some unpleasant life experiences for themselves. This only shows that we can't escape grief no matter how hard we try. Moreover, nor should we want to, as it often changes us into a better, more fulfilled person.

Other cultural factors indicate that grief is not valued in this society. Just look at most company bereavement policies if they exist at all. The norm would be three days off for the arrangements and the funeral. You may be granted an additional two days. This amount of time is woefully inadequate. These days often only apply to very close relatives. For example, your mother, father, sister, brother, grandparents and maybe in-laws would be on the list. Aunts and uncles frequently are not included. Certainly close friends, who for some are like family, are rarely if ever mentioned.

If grief becomes more valued and acknowledged, the rules of exclusion may change to accommodate anyone having a significant impact on your life. Providing a sufficient amount of time to manage this stage of grief would be a welcome change in policy. You could infer that there is nothing needed after this initial grieving period. Currently most policies don't match our human need. I wonder how many sick days are due to grief reactions. The researchers at the Grief Recovery Institute, a nonprofit educational foundation wondered that as well. They undertook to measure how grief affects U.S. businesses in dollars and cents. They determined in the "Grief Index", the death of a loved one costs business in lost productivity $37.5 billion a year. Other losses due to grief cost billions of dollars as well. If nothing else gets our attention, this should!! Businesses need to wake up and make changes to their practices to accommodate their staff's needs that are going through this difficult time. The benefits would surely outweigh the costs overall and foster a caring work environment for their employees.

Encouraging the use or initiating employee assistance programs would be greatly beneficial. More education is required for managers to identify the symptoms of grief exhibited by their staff. A shift in the culture of many organizations is required to more effectively deal with grief experienced by their staff. Anger, tension, irritability, and low morale are only a few behaviors that could be contributed to grief reactions.

Progressive companies should develop other creative ways to deal with employee stress. What used to be called "sick rooms" could now be used for other purposes. These rooms decorated in a warm homey theme could be a place where staff could go if experiencing a difficult time. They may not need to leave work if there was a safe place to go. An attitude of acceptance in an organization would be essential for this practice to work. Often the diminished work capacity that a staff member may be experiencing is associated with the loss that may have been suffered many months before. The effects of grief may have an impact on performance for quite some time when not dealt with appropriately. Management and staff need to work together to change the organization culture of our workplaces.

We have no way in our society of telling that we have sustained a loss that has profoundly affected us. They do in other cultures. Many cultures openly display their grief. Wearing black for a mourning period is a familiar symbol that some cultures display. This symbol is respected and has empathy associated with it that supports the grieving individual. They do not feel isolated, as they know their community understands and supports them.

Our society values quick and easy solutions to any problem and that includes emotions. Baby boomers have been told the pursuit of happiness and instant gratification can be ours. If it is quicker, it is better. Let's not confuse efficiency with effectiveness. It doesn't work with grief. To make matters even worse, we believe hurt and pain is something to be controlled and is not tolerated. We mistakenly apply this same ideology to grief. There must be something wrong if we hurt. The term closure is used frequently when dealing with a loved one's death. It is such a ridiculous term to use in this circumstance. It is not a business transaction that we are "closing". We can't take two aspirins and be better in the morning after the "closure" of the funeral has taken place. We want to believe that we can live in a pain-free society. Many options have been available to this generation to manage most pain. There is nothing that exists to manage or avoid the pain of grief. This is where the biggest changes in our culture can occur. Grief is pain and needs to be acknowledged and felt.

There is also some discrimination felt by the bereaved that certain losses are viewed by our society as more difficult than others. No one but the person who has suffered the loss can describe the depth of the emotion they are feeling. But as a society, we tend to decide who deserves either more sorrow by the grieving or time taken with the process. Have you ever witnessed the reaction to someone's loss and thought to yourself " They were only his or her stepfather" for example. This type of judgment frequently experienced does nothing to assist the bereaved in their grief. It will drive them many times to isolate themselves further, feeling that their experience is not something that will be viewed as significant by those around them.

Your friends and family most likely don't know how to help you through this time. We must all be willing to learn to help each other through this life event.

The people around you may seem uncomfortable dealing with your feelings after you lose someone. Often they're dealing with their own feelings about the loss and approach you with trepidation. They could be afraid of hurting you more or breaking down themselves and not being strong for you. Also they could feel there's nothing they could say to make you feel better. People sometimes fear their awkwardness will embarrass them. They do not want you to misunderstand or reject them. What they don't understand is you just need them to listen without judgment. You too may feel uncomfortable sharing your thoughts and feelings. We need to show each other and understand that most anything is all right to say if it is said with love and support for the other person. It takes trust, courage, and time to open this subject of conversation.

Talking about the deceased is often avoided as people think that will make you feel worse. But talking about the loved one can often be of great comfort. It brings the deceased to life through shared stories and remembrances. Your positive reaction to these stories will encourage others to talk more.

Our culture seems to have forgotten the special importance of the funeral. Funerals are the rituals or ceremonies people engage in immediately after the person has died. The decision about any rituals should be what to do and not if we should do it. Not having some ritual will most likely be regretted in the future. They are an important part of the grieving process. How this event is handled is significant to how those grieving will begin their mourning.

The support we receive from family and friends is of great comfort to those of us who have suffered a loss. This may not be apparent until you have experienced a loss. The strength of a community offering sympathy and warm remembrances should not be underestimated. The way the grief stricken deal with support tells others how to help in the future. If no visitation is offered, the bereaved are indicating that close friends aren't needed. This may not be the case, but it can be the message. The support you provide by going to a funeral or visitation if it is offered will not go unnoticed by the bereaved.

After the funeral, our culture has expectations about how we will blend back into daily life. There may be more time allowed by society for grieving, if the deceased was very close or if the death occurred under extraordinary circumstances. But in either case the time is relatively short and there is an expectation that things will be back to normal pretty quickly.

Emotional expressions of grief are not usually well received. Society encourages us to bury these feelings in public. We find it difficult to deal with the extended period of mourning people need. Grieving never really ends. You are affected by this loss for the rest of your life. You may find new meaning to what the death has meant to you but the journey never ends – it just changes as you go through it.

Unfortunately, in the near future we will encounter many close friends and colleagues that will be beginning this journey. Let's start the dialogue so that we can be more prepared to help those before they experience this for the first time. This would increase our understanding of each other as we travel through life and all its ups and downs. I believe in the power of shared experiences.

A tidal surge of grief will be hitting the baby boomers soon. Despite my trepidation, apprehension and alarm I hope that we can deal with this phenomenon. Certainly, the experience of grief is not new. But the difference is the numbers to be affected in a relatively short time are so great for this generation.

Going through this together may bring new perspective to our lives and how we live the rest of our lives. If handled properly, there could be many good outcomes to this tragic time in our lives.

Let's hang onto each other and use all our resources,

the best of which will be each other- to help, listen, and provide support to all who need it. Many will become more spiritual and discover a new richness in their lives.

Understanding grief is the first step in making this time in our lives more bearable. It will be less frightening and confusing if we all share our experiences with grief. This sharing and outward expression of grief will be new to this culture. Who but the baby boomers would be more appropriate to show our children how to deal with life's losses? Let's set an example by our actions during these difficult times.

The baby boomers have changed many cultural aspects. Collectively, we have power and influence and this is the time to stand up and get noticed.

Chapter Four

RELATIONSHIPS

O ur relationships are the most important aspect of our lives. Other aspects seem to pale in comparison. The state of our relationships affects all areas of our lives.

The depths of those ties enrich our lives. The caring, love, compassion, sensitivity, and laughter that we share with the people we love bind us to them in an indescribable manner. So when these people leave us, we feel empty. We need to learn how to heal without being too deeply scarred.

When our parents are alive, we know there is a place on this earth that we can always call home. Our parents give us an unconditional love that cannot be duplicated by any other relationship. They can often be taken for granted but we never lose our initial attachment to our parents.

Supporting each other through loss is one way we all can benefit. By our actions, we can teach others how to help us deal with our pain. We should not hide. Shutting ourselves off from friends and family will not ease our suffering.

The relationship with our loved one is remembered in great detail. Initially we focus on remembering all their good qualities and the good times. The memories bring many tears as we remember the good times we shared. We realize these will not occur again.

Some people actively block fond remembrances, because it is too painful. Others try to remember, firmly embedding those memories in their mind so to never lose them. They may also ask friends and family to share their memories.

The dangerous part is that sometimes we can put the deceased on a pedestal. Everyone has faults and no relationship is perfect. The cloudy areas of our memory may make us remember a person who never existed. Make an effort to remember the good and the bad about the relationship. Both elements should be included even in the best of relationships.

We loved a person who was human with all the normal frailties. We don't have to be perfect to be loved. You loved them for all of their qualities. Moreover, they loved you too! This doesn't mean the person you remember was weak. Remember the whole person. Although it may be painful to remember difficult times, all memories at this point are painful. Nevertheless, remember this important person, warts and all. Laughing and crying over memories brings the loved one closer.

At funerals you may wondered to yourself, "Whom are they talking about?" This comment reflects that a distorted description of your loved one has been depicted.. I'm sure you would want to reflect the whole person.

Once we have a clear perspective of the person, the relationship doesn't stop there. We still have a relationship. Though the relationship won't evolve the way that it used to, it can change with you.

You may develop rituals of remembering that comfort you through the years. Some people have small areas in their home with mementos of the person and perhaps even light a candle occasionally or some other meaningful symbolic gesture.

Spirituality plays a big part in how you relate to the person after they are gone. Some people do believe the spirit lives on in a very literal sense and the person is watching over them. In this way they still feel a connection to their loved one. They recount experiences that show them the evidence that someone is close. I have personally experienced this. It gives immeasurable comfort to believe the person continues to be close in some form even though you can't touch them. Some have reported actually having short conversations with past relatives. We must decide for ourselves what we believe on this subject. How you deal with these spiritual matters is intensely private but can make a significant impact on how you manage your grief in the days ahead.

Another way our loved one lingers is through stories from others. You will learn different aspects of your loved one. It is interesting to know other facets of the person you loved and increases your memories and love for them.

Your relationship with friends and family is crucial. They often provide the support you need to face the world again. We need to be open to that comfort. Let your family and friends know that you need their support and let them know how they can help you through this difficult time. Understanding your loss is the most important information that your friends need to help you. Without that, they have no perspective on what you are going through. You must communicate this information to them to ensure they understand the depth of the loss that you are feeling. In my case, it was obvious to everyone that my mother and I were very close. My pain was obvious. That won't always be the case. They will be unsure of how to help you, but those who care will be eager to learn, if you teach them.

You may feel like hiding from them, but share your pain so they can also learn from this difficult time. It is with the caring shown and feeling the pain together that we will all heal and grow.

I had many supportive friends, and they were there when I cried, laughed, got angry and sad. My friends were an immeasurable support and comfort to me when my mother died. They were there for me and made it easy for me to tell them what I needed. Even when I didn't want to do anything they would not allow me to hide. I think they felt my pain with me, which showed me how connected we really are. There was no time limit on their support.

It became obvious that I had taken such friendship for granted. They were the anchors in the storm o
that had struck me like a lightening bolt. I couldn
managed without them.

I was extremely lucky to have such supportive fi
Friends do not always react in the way I have des
Many people are uncomfortable with this issue n
ter how close they feel to you. If you run up agai
reluctance, there are other available avenues of su

It may be hard for your friends at first. Your
may be unaware of the changes going on in you

sciousness but will start to gradually notice changes in you. Sometimes friendship cannot tolerate these changes and does not survive. However, often the changes do not come about immediately. It takes some time for this process to take place. Your perspective of the world has shifted, and our reaction to it will be different.

You may feel the changes are happening to you but aren't yet apparent to those around you. This was my experience. I had a vague notion I was looking at life differently, but it was some time before friends said they noticed a change. They were warm and supportive and we discussed life issues that we never would have in the past. My experience and change had caused a change in them as well. Psychologists say that you can't change someone else; you can only change yourself. However, changes that occur with you may have an influence over those close to you. This was a good example of that psychology.

It is inevitable that the relationships we have with those around us will change as we change. It cannot be helped. The friends around us will see the change in us and have to adapt to this new person they now have as their friend. This is one way we can assist others to understand what they will be facing one day. Just as you look at life differently, you will also look at your relationships differently.

I changed the way I viewed my various relationships. I became aware of the wonderful and diverse people I had the privilege to call my friends. For the first time I realized the richness that these friends added to my life.

I also became less judgmental than I had in the past. People no longer had to fit into my preconceived moulds. They could be who they were and I could accept them and be grateful for their friendship. I found myself cherishing the time I spent with them. I have tried to stay "still" at times to relish these special moments.

My best friend, Barb, was a constant source of support always acknowledging the pain she knew I would feel when certain situations arose. Her understanding of my relationship with my mother and the effect her death had on me is revealed in this poem she wrote for me.

MOTHER LOVE
By Barb Dudley

I'm so glad we're friends, I always think of you,
And it makes me sad to think about the grief that
you've been through
A mother is special; she can't be replaced,
She's the foundation on which your whole life is based
Her gift will live on, and guide your life now,
You must follow in her footsteps; she's shown you how.

61

It's such an enduring love, that it won't go away,
You'll feel it and use it in your life every day.
When you look down deep into your beautiful eyes,
You'll know that a Mother's love never dies.
In all that you are, and all that you do,
You'll feel her love shining down on you.

I truly believe I was blessed having many friends and I don't hesitate to tell them that on a regular basis.

Other relationships that often go through changes are with the family left by the deceased. It has the potential for positive change as well as some negative effects.

The roles managed by the deceased need to be filled by someone else. This can create stress and sadness for those trying to fill these shoes. These roles can be housekeeping tasks or the emotional roles that now have to be filled within the family unit. Both are difficult to fill as you try to live up to the way things had been done in the past. It may be that the role is not immediately assumed, leaving a distinct emptiness in the family in relation to that responsibility. These are the days of adjustment. New patterns will develop to fill the void left by the loss.

Closeness often unites a family when they have suffered a loss. They feel the need to band together to support each other. Each is dependent on the other to maintain the integrity of the support. This closeness may strengthen the family in this process. Individual relationships may also be enhanced as they travel this path of grief together. Previously unknown strengths of family members may also come to light. Navigating this emotional time may bring many families closer, allowing them to show more love and empathy towards each other.

Learning that others have qualities previously undetected might change how we look at our other relationships. We may need to look more deeply to see their special qualities. A renewed value is placed on all our relationships as we learn how fragile life can be.

While feeling the loss and grief, we realize how important people are in our lives. It causes us to review what priorities were important in the past and re-consider what is important now. Our baby boomer generation has focused on accumulating "things". Grief will significantly impact that way of thinking. Things can always be replaced but people can't. Perhaps this way of thinking has started to occur. Some of this generation are now "simplifying" their lives and connecting to a richer and more satisfying lifestyle. Grief can be the slap in our face that wakes us up and makes us question what we have valued in the past and what we have taken for granted.

Despite knowing that our parents will die one day, the reality cannot be grasped until you face the event. It brings you one generation closer to your own death and those of close friends. Facing your own mortality is difficult. It requires soul-searching about your life and purpose on this earth. The questioning of what we are doing and how it affects others may trigger life-altering decisions. What happens when many baby boomers are going through this exercise at the same time? Major changes in our culture most likely will occur and this may be a key factor in changing the priorities of our generation. Recent interest in spirituality and other venues concerned with the "unknown" may be just the tip of the iceberg.

Starting a new relationship is also different. We may be more in touch with our own needs now, which will influence who comes into our lives. We're often more open to people than we were in the past. We may see a quality in them that we now feel is important. We may be drawn to people who experienced something similar and have connected to their spiritual side. Through this process, we can enrich our lives with new friends who add a new dimension to our lives. This is a wonderful result of a terrible experience. Positive outcomes can result.

People will go through these changes in their own way or perhaps not at all, but change is the result of the grief process. A powerful initiator for change is living in a world that has been shaken up and totally different.

Changed relationships can be a welcome, healing outcome to a terrible life event. The support we receive can be offered to others when they experience a similar loss.

CHAPTER FIVE

FUNERAL RITUALS

Funeral rituals serve a valuable purpose in the grieving process. It is the first essential step in moving toward healing the pain. Religious people are not the only ones to benefit from the experience. Anyone can make a funeral meaningful for their family and themselves. This allows an opportunity to remember the person who is no longer with us, in a meaningful way.

Making the funeral arrangements distracts those starting the grieving process, but this is the positive side. To be forced into another train of thought is like being thrown a life preserver when the shock, disbelief, disorientation, and sadness are overwhelming. Your mind needs some rest from the pain and all the funeral decisions send your thoughts in another direction. Funerals offer a reprieve as the many details serve as a distraction from the pain. During this acute grief, it seems a good distraction until you have the physical and emotional reserves to handle it.

At this time, your mind is probably not functioning at it's best. As confused as you may be, your decisions are vitally important as you get only one opportunity to honor your loved one as you would like.

We do feel we are doing something meaningful for the person we have lost. This is a gratifying feeling, as it will be the last thing we will do for them .We want our actions and decisions to have meaning.

We need to feel sadness to start the journey and funerals offer a safe place for those emotions to be felt, embraced, and expressed. You feel more comfortable here surrounded by the people that love you. A touch of a friend's hand or a hug can give immeasurable comfort. It's better to be sitting with someone grieving, feeling anxious and uncomfortable, than not sitting with them. It's one of the few socially acceptable times to show these raw emotions. Take advantage of this time, as it doesn't last for long, as you will find out!!!!

Funerals are just the start of your long journey. It is your opportunity to honor your loved one and start the grieving process. You must take care of yourself and not rush through the process. Doing things efficiently will not necessarily be an effective grieving or healing path. Funerals are often "gotten through" instead of partici- pated in and made more meaningful for the bereaved. People often don't grasp the importance of the ceremony involved with the funeral. At a palliative care conference I attended, Dr. Alan Wolfelt said, "when words are inad- equate, have ceremony".

Funerals allow us to say good-bye to our loved one's presence in the world. It is when we are first acutely aware that we will be living our life without that person. Denial is difficult when faced with funeral arrangements. There are many different types of ceremonies that provide ways to say goodbye to your loved one. If we miss these cer- emonies, we miss the support and soothing effect they offer.

The word closure has been used a lot, often in refer- ence to the funeral ceremony. Although it does allow us to say good-bye and share memories, it does not close the book on that person's life or the grieving process. It is somewhat insulting to think that we just close the door on the person we have loved. We are still a long way away from incorporating this reality into our everyday life. It does allow us to move from loving the person in the present to loving them in a state of separateness. The ritual of saying good-bye is an important first step in the process.

The spiritual aspect of this ritual will often provide comfort when you are looking for answers. Your own spiritual beliefs may surface, because of this tragic incident, in ways you would not expect. It will also help if you believe your loved one is in a better place.

Ceremonies include both formal and informal customs and behaviors. All of these customs however are intended to say good-bye but at the same time pay your respect and honor your loved one.

Ceremonies rely on symbols for their powerful effect. These can range from the flowers, music, and donations to candles, pictures, keeping a journal, dedicating objects and even naming children after the loved one. These activities and symbols help sustain us through the funeral and for the months and years to come when we need strength to deal with grief.

You will want your loved one's wishes to be respected. It is never easy thinking of our own death, despite our age. Even older people don't want to discuss their own funeral. It is difficult for anyone to face his or her own mortality. They will need encouragement from you to share these thoughts and wishes

But we often have no idea what our loved one would like as a remembrance. You will have to sort through your memory, to remember even any insignificant statement or opinion expressed that might give you a clue as to their wishes.

Having not had this discussion with my mother, I would advise you to talk about it. It is a difficult conversation for some, but worth having. The point is to honor this person and it's difficult to do if you haven't talked about it. Not knowing creates more difficult decision-making when you are in a vulnerable state. Not knowing only adds more emotional stress to your life.

Some basic issues to be considered are cremation or burial, open or closed casket, flowers or choice of donations, the funeral home they would like and where they would like to be buried. Having answered these questions will allow you to honour their wishes. Your main focus is to do things the way they would have wanted them done.

The more you know their preferences, the better you can handle the situation. This gives you a level of comfort at the beginning of the process. You can show your love and respect for the person and avoid the stress of making decisions you may not feel comfortable with later.

The only easy decision for me was the choice of cemetery. My mother and I had been to a cemetery looking for the gravesite of a friend. She commented she liked this cemetery. It had a lovely view of the city and would be a lovely place for family to visit. The first thing I did was to go to that cemetery. I requested the grave on the highest point of the hill. It was at least one decision made I was sure would please my mother.

By their sheer staggering numbers, baby boomers have been used to getting their own way. Show some individuality and make funerals meaningful. You don't have to fit into a predetermined preformed mold. Funerals can follow any format. The setting for the service does not have to be in a church for example. A special place can add a unique touch to the ceremony. People will remember it for years to come.

It is essential for a meaningful ceremony that the decisions related to the funeral reflect the uniqueness of the deceased and the family. Traditionally the funeral occurs just a few days after the death. The resultant pace with which these decisions must be made often leads to hasty decisions that cannot be given the thought they deserve. Why does this process have to occur so quickly? We should be able to take the time needed to organize a meaningful ceremony.

You also have to decide how much you want to participate in this event. Saying goodbye to someone you love is always difficult. The ceremonies are more meaningful if you actively contribute to their development and execution. When we take part in this ritual, we are openly engaging our pain and starting to move forward. Participating does not have to mean speaking at the ceremony if this makes you feel uncomfortable. There are many ways to participate. Saying goodbye should be an experience we can feel was a fitting tribute to our loved one.

Anything is a good idea that allows you to feel closer to the loved one or to honor their memory. There is no right or wrong. It only needs to feel good to you. Do not feel forced into decisions that make you feel uncomfortable. It is as individual as you and the person you loved. The pitfall is doing what everyone says you should, just because "it has always been done that way".

The degree to which you become involved in the ceremony is entirely up to you. Depending on the funeral home and the clergy you select, this may or may not be encouraged. It takes strength to make all of these choices but it will be worth it if you personalize the service to reflect your loved one. You know what feels best and will give the funeral meaning and richness. Do not be discouraged from doing what you would like to do. A family member or close friends are the only ones that can make some personal decisions. Picking the clothes your loved one wears, notes or momentos to be placed in the casket, pallbearers, the grave marker and the music to accompany the service are decisions that attempt to reflect your loved one's wishes.

Difficult decisions will be meaningful in the end and

you will be happy that you had the courage to make them. Opening the casket, the amount of visitation time, the degree of your participation and choices regarding the service or memorial are just some of the more difficult decisions.

After the funeral, you don't want to feel you had no control in the way it was handled. You don't want to miss the opportunity to say goodbye in the your own way. You may want to choose a balance between observer and contributor. Only you can decide what is right for you.

There is not an easy resolution to these decisions. Many family members will often be trying to reach a consensus regarding how the ritual should be conducted.

Emotions running high and differing expectations will almost certainly conflict. Lack of knowledge regarding the deceased wishes will increase the tension. Try not to allow disagreements to come between family and friends. You will need each other in the days to come.

Communication about the wishes and expectations of those involved will help avoid the divergence of opinions getting out of control. Awareness is the first step to avoid such discord. Acknowledging the need for understanding, sensitivity, acceptance, cooperation, and mutual respect is the key.

Remember the goal of this process. You are making decisions about someone who has meant a great deal to all of you. Focus on respecting this person's memory the best way you can and helping each other deal with the loss.

Funerals provide us with support and a special day of remembering. Having people who were linked to your loved one offers special possibilities. Often there are friends of the deceased that you haven't seen in a long time. This reunion is often bittersweet, as you wish this meeting were occurring for a different reason. But there is comfort in the collective presence of friends and family. The mutual feelings of love for the departed encourage those left behind. It intensifies the respect that people show to the family.

Memories are shared at funerals in various ways. There is the formal eulogy. Many close friends can frequently offer this. It can be planned or people at the funeral can be asked if they would like to share their memories. People are happy to do something that will lessen your pain. The most effective eulogy is based on personal knowledge and adds a depth of meaning to the ceremony. This process validates your loved one's importance, bringing them closer to you.

Pictures are becoming a focal point of many visitations and funerals. Many people will make a collage and often have an enlarged picture on or near the casket. With computers being such an integral part of the baby boomer's lives, they can be useful in this regard. One visitation I attended recently had digital pictures on a computer screen that constantly changed. It quickly became the focal point of the room with people gathering around. This also encourages story telling which can be very comforting to the bereaved family members. With the technology now available there are many unique ways to use this to make the funeral service and visitation more meaningful to everyone.

The memories shared at this time are varied. Your mind travels from recent memories and back many years in successive thoughts. Family and friends recount additional memories. It's wonderful to hear people talking of the person you have loved so much. Shared grief is a powerful force. Memories come out in informal areas such as the visitation or at the family home after the service. Have people share their memories in a written form that you can keep and refer to later and at your leisure. People will be happy to do something for you that is comforting.

Many people attending funerals feel uncomfortable with your grief and do not want to further upset you. So there is a chance you will miss an opportunity to hear their stories if you do not take the lead. Don't be afraid to ask people to tell you stories about your loved one.

Sometimes it takes your permission for them to open up and share the most wonderful tales.

Your friend's support during this grueling time is a treasured gift. You are already riding waves of emotions. The outpouring of love from friends can be overwhelming. You see in concrete terms how important friends are to you.

Even though apprehension surrounds the funeral process, it is important you do what you feel comfortable with, as this is your opportunity to produce a ceremony to honor your loved one.

Allow your emotions to come and don't let the event distract you from those feelings. People will often try to avoid the good-bye because they fear they will become emotional. Please don't miss this important occasion. You can be distracted by the companionship of close friends that are reunited for the funeral. Try not to misread your own need for support during the funeral process. This is a time of disconnection and change.

The result should be a warm and gratifying remembrance of the funeral. Many factors can interfere with your ability to clearly remember the event. There are some ways to help keep that memory alive. Keep as mementos the passages that are read at the service. Some funeral homes will provide an audiotape if requested. You may not be aware of all the people who attended. Review the guest book and letters received after the event. You can remind yourself who demonstrated their support to you and your family. You will be amazed at what you forget about this significant life event.

Though the funeral is the first step towards your journey of healing, it takes place in a short time frame with an abundance of varied emotions. Take this opportunity to show your respect for your loved one. Make it count.

CHAPTER SIX

WHAT NOT TO DO

The next two chapters offer some hints that might make your journey more bearable. It is up to you what advice you accept and practice. All suggestions come from the experience of those who have learned the hard way.

If you do nothing else, try not to suppress your feelings during the grieving process. Don't be ashamed of mourning the death of someone you loved. It takes too much energy to deny that you are going through a difficult time. You are reacting to an event that will change your life so let out those feelings in any way that feels comfortable. Feelings will be unpredictable in their frequency and intensity. Try not to fight them when they emerge. You need to feel the pain before you will heal.

It is often difficult to deal with the expectations others place on us. Each loss we encounter will bring it's own unique reaction. Often we are hard on ourselves if we don't feel the way we expect to in this situation. These expectations may come from the comments of well meaning friends, family or may even be self-imposed. They may differ depending on the geographical or cultural community. All you can do is accept your feelings and don't judge whether you are feeling enough or too much. You are the only one who knows exactly what you are feeling.

We can often do more harm to ourselves in this respect than anyone can do to us. You are emotionally vulnerable and must be clear about what you can and, more importantly, what you cannot do at this time.

Many people think they can escape the pain. This is another version of keeping your feelings inside and not dealing with them as they arise. This does not have the effect that you expect.

One example would be to try to stop the thoughts constantly on your mind. Don't try to escape them. The emotions you may be able to bury now most likely will surface at an inappropriate time in the future. At some time in your life you may have done this. One method is to vary your routine so you reduce the triggers present. You imagine your mind will be free of those invading thoughts and you can escape. Think again. Why not deal with the feelings as they come?

There is an irresistible temptation to cocoon yourself when you are in pain. This is one temptation to be avoided. You certainly can fluctuate between wanting some time alone and wanting closeness with others. Making constant excuses why you are unavailable will soon raise your friend's alarm. You will only deprive yourself of the friends and family, who are there to support you. Keeping yourself cut off from the world will only make your eventual return more difficult.

It is natural to hide the pain from yourself and others and try to deny its existence. You might stop activities that were previously important to you. It is often hard to carry on in a world so drastically altered. It can be quite easy to make changes to our daily routine. Go back to at least some of your regular activities. This will bring some normalcy to your life. The bottom line is not to become a recluse in your pain.

Another escape is going somewhere unfamiliar. An example of this is to go on vacation or any place not resembling home. There is a desire to create new memories that are not associated with pain. The fact remains that you cannot run from the pain. It travels with you and doesn't take up much room in your suitcase. And if you run to unfamiliar surroundings with your difficult emotions, you won't have the comfort of your own home, friends and family nearby.

During this time your mind won't function with it's normal acuity. Your world has been turned upside down and your vision of the future is significantly impaired – this is an incredible understatement. You are the best judge of when you feel in control again.

Decisions about significant issues should be delayed until thinking that is more rational can kick in. Taking it easy is the order for the day.

What to do with your loved one's possessions requires thoughtful consideration and should not be rushed. Others may have a part in this decision and they should be encouraged to go slowly. Items that you might think should be given away may not be viewed in the same light in a few months. By holding on to too many items in the beginning you won't go wrong if you change your mind in the future. However, if you discard in haste you won't be able to reverse your decision in the future.

Life will look differently to you in the future than it does now. It's impossible to know what will be the best decision to make for the future. So just don't make it, yet. Only you can determine when the mist on your brain and senses has lifted enough to make appropriate decisions. Step back from this for a while and wait until the fog clears.

You may be invited to a social function and are not sure whether to attend. Follow your gut feeling. Don't be afraid to decline invitations you receive if you are physically or emotionally not able to handle the activity. You can always politely decline and friends that really care will understand. Don't be forced into something you are not comfortable doing. It is strictly your decision how to handle these situations. You are the best judge.

Being with people in any situation can often take a great deal of energy on your part. If you are feeling like you have to be "normal" for your friends or family, this "Oscar performance" can really tire you out. Out society almost expects this play-acting on our part, which is unfortunate. Putting on the face of normalcy when you are burdened with grief is extremely difficult but is done all the time. If you are around friends that allow you to feel and express whatever it is you are feeling you will not have to expend this energy to put up a front.

Even though a loved one's possessions can produce a painful response, don't try to avoid the memories. Man ways have been tried. Some people avoid memories t putting away pictures, cleaning out closets too soon aft the death, selling precious belongings and giving aw belongings. These activities remove all reminders of t loved one. The memories don't go away no matter wl you do. There can also be some guilt experienced if th remembrances are removed. You are still dealing with your own fresh wounds of grief.

Most want to feel self-sufficient. But rejecting the assistance of others is definitely a mistake. There will be many things you will have to do on your own. Confirmation that you are experiencing a normal reaction to a tragic event will make you feel so much better about your handling of this period.

You may find other strategies that have not been successful in relieving your distress during this volatile passage in life. Pass on any information learned to friends that has or hasn't helped you so they can learn from your experience.

CHAPTER SEVEN

WHAT TO DO

There are many things you can do to help yourself through this time. What will work for you will be as individual as you are. Don't hesitate to try anything you think will help. There are many ways through this life experience. Nothing is wrong if it provides comfort. It will be up to each of us to find the way through this emotional maze ourselves.

Talking is the most important activity you can engage in to deal with your raw emotions. You need to talk and talk and talk and talk – and whom you talk to really isn't important! What is important is the person's willingness to listen again and again. You need to find someone who will be there to listen to you for as long as you need.

Recounting the circumstances around the death is

repeated often and discussed in great detail. It seems strangely important to remember every part of the situation that led up to the death. I recited the story more times than I could count. The people listening to me had incredible patience for this repetition. I know this reiteration is an important part of the process. I suspect it helps you incorporate the situation into your reality.

Talking can take several avenues during this time of pain and healing. Expressing feelings is one area, but talking about the deceased is another. It is often not easily dealt with by those close to you, as they fear that talking about the person you have lost will upset you. Don't allow their fear to stop you from bringing your loved one's name into conversations. This usually brings comfort. You can teach by example. Often people don't understand your need to speak about your loved one.

There are many different arenas talking can take place. n the best support comes from your family, friends, neighbours. They are an invaluable source of love support. Assist them to help you by telling what asce you are seeking from them. Friends are often ent to say anything, not wanting to upset you fur so let them know what you need at this time in your ng. Unless you advise them, people will not know to comfort you. They may not instinctively know needs. The truth is, people experiencing grief are grateful when their friends recognize this major change in their life.

Realize that help is out there and if you make use of this assistance it doesn't mean you're a weak person. Support from a professional may be the most comfortable situation for some and counselors are available in most communities. All discussions with a health professional are confidential. This is often a concern. The key to getting the most out of a therapy session is to be honest about your feelings. If you're not honest, you are cheating yourself. Allow the therapist to see the big picture, including any thoughts that you think make you look insane. There will be many of those thoughts I can assure you! The therapist will not be surprised and it will be comforting to know that this is a normal part of the process. Don't be afraid to say exactly what is on your mind. You won't shock a therapist believe me. They have heard it all before.

Bereavement groups are available in many communities. The need has recently been identified for groups of baby boomers losing their parents. Groups specifically for children and spouses are also offered. These groups are useful for anyone experiencing any loss. Sharing this experience with others can offer validation to the feelings you have on a daily basis. There is reassurance in knowing that others know and can empathize with how you feel.

The written word is the best way to express feelings for many. This private activity allows the flow of thoughts into words on paper. Some people can only express an honest expression of sadness, loss and grief in a written form. If you are more comfortable with this write whenever you feel the urge. Keep a journal with you to be ready when the urge moves you.

While all of this is going on, be sure to take good care of yourself. Your physical and emotional well being is very important at this time. It can significantly affect how you deal with your grief on a daily basis.

Maintain your diet and get enough sleep and exercise. Let your friends and families help you in these activities. If someone wants to make you dinner, accept his or her offer. Sometimes even this simple task can seem monumental.

You may experience physical symptoms during the grieving process. Some of these could include stomach problems, headaches, weakness, chest pain, muscle aches, dizziness, lightheadedness, and anxiety. Many of these can often be resolved by simply taking better care of yourself. But there are also medical remedies for some of the symptoms. Consult your physician for the best course of treatment for you.

One of the most common symptom of grieving is the inability to sleep or to stay asleep. Our minds race with a multitude of thoughts that prevents us from getting to sleep. Nightmares commonly will wake us from our sleep and make it impossible to resume our sleep. Not receiving enough sleep does not assist your mental functioning. Sleep can be elusive so if you feel tired in the middle of the day, take a nap if that option is available to you.

Medication that addresses the lack of sleep issue should be used judiciously and under physician's supervision. Soaking baths, soothing music and warm milk can be a substitute when required in the future. There are also some natural sleep aids that can be found in health food stores to assist with sleeping difficulties. Anti-anxiety medication also falls into this category. They undoubtedly relieve immobilizing symptoms, but they should not be used to dull your emotions. The use of any substance should be discussed with your physician. Quickly comes the time that these should be used less and less and the person starts to rely on his or her own coping skills and support.

You may sleep too much. Sleeping often, for long periods of time and not feeling refreshed may be a sign of depression. These symptoms are just as important as not enough sleep and needs to be addressed by a physician for the proper medical care.

Thoughts of your loved one can invade your mind relentlessly at first and for some time after the death. Your mind feels overcrowded with thoughts racing in your head. It takes an incredible amount of energy to deal with these every day. Try to distract yourself with an activity you enjoy.

Now is the time to allow yourself some time for your hobbies or other activities you enjoy, even for just a little while. Any hobby will give your mind a much-deserved rest. Horses were my lifelines when I went through this period. It was one of the only times I could participate in an activity without thoughts of my mother coming into my mind. The constancy of those thoughts wore me down.

Participating in activities that make you feel good is a great idea during this time. For some putting their hands in the soil and tending a garden can take them to another place in their mind. But also be aware that it takes some strength to say no to activities that you would prefer to avoid.

Only you can judge whether you need distractions. Participating in activities you enjoy can only have a positive outcome. Doing something with your hands is often soothing—knitting, painting, housework, or doing a jigsaw puzzle. Listening to your favorite music is also comforting. Give yourself permission to do something that brings joy to your life.

Focusing on someone else may help you escape your thoughts. It can also give you a great lift. You may be able to do something for a friend or even a needy stranger. You could also give something back to your community by volunteering. You will feel good about yourself as well as turning off the spotlight on your sorrow.

To those grieving keeping the person close is a prime concern. Many objects in our possession will help achieve this purpose but there are other ways as well. Dealing with this heavy blow involves the realization this has really happened. Reliving memories we have of our loved one helps us realize that memories are all we have left. But having those items near us helps to cement the new relationship we will have with our loved one.

Photographs can tell a story of a person's life, if put together in some format. An album can bring back memories as you move through their life in pictures. Scattered around the house, they can comfort those dealing with their grief. Pictures become extremely important to the grieving. I know that I couldn't get enough pictures around me. I was constantly looking for more.

This is a good reason to take many pictures and stop ducking behind a door whenever someone points a camera in your direction. Of course, my mother was the picture taker in our family, which means that she was not in many of them. I have since changed my ways and avidly take pictures now. I know that someday these may be very important to someone I love.

Pictures and videotapes help us to remember the person we have lost and remind us of situations and events that we shared. As painful as these memories may be at first, they will eventually turn into warm reminders of our loved one and the life we shared. It is not unusual to look at these pictures or videos repeatedly. In this computer age, they can be incorporated into our lives as screensavers. It is difficult to understand how all this helps the healing but I can assure you it does.

You can keep some keepsakes to feel they are always with you. A ring could be put on a necklace. Clothes and jewelry worn may bring comfort. The smell of clothes or a particular perfume can also trigger powerful memories. Sitting in a chair, which was previously a favorite one, can have an unbelievably soothing effect on someone enveloped by grief. Just being near the belongings of your loved one can bring you comfort.

Memorials are another way for the bereaved to make a statement that this loss is significant in their lives. A grave marker is only one way for you to express your feelings. Visiting the cemetery either regularly or on special days is a ritual many incorporate into their lives. The Internet has many web sites that are a tribute to their loved one. Power point presentations about a person's life can be shared easily even through email messages. Memorials can be any ritual that comforts you in celebrating a special life.

You can create some rituals in your daily routine that serve as a memorial to the deceased. Many people light candles, say a special prayer in memory, or even create a special toast in honor of your loved one. Another popular idea is having an area of the house include items that represent who they were or held some significance to them.

The purpose of these activities is to keep the memory and spirit of the deceased alive in your mind and heart. So do whatever comforts you.

Many aspects of our daily lives can produce disturbing thoughts. Movies that appear on television in today's world often have upsetting and distressing subject matter. I found I was very sensitive to this type of television programming suddenly. I would not have predicted this reaction to a television show. Try to avoid any subject matter that is disturbing to you at this point in your healing process.

There will be times you will want and need to be alone. This is sometimes an impossible task. You need to allow time for the reflection that is part of the process. This is an important first step. Allow yourself permission to explore the spiritual aspects that grieving opens for some. You need the opportunity to explore your thoughts, feelings, memories, hopes and dreams of the future. It is part of getting through the waves of grief you experience.

When special days bring anxiety and dread you will need to be your own barometer. If you need some distraction, call a close family member or friend and share your feelings about the day. You could also use the day to celebrate their memory by doing something they liked to do or you did with them. Visiting the grave or a church is not unusual for many but will depend on your comfort at the time. Keeping up familiar rituals offer some structure to these difficult days. You will get through them more easily each year.

It needs to be mentioned that the process you are going through won't feel as painful in the future as it does now. You may ask, "What is the time frame involved"? There is no magic formula to know when the pain will diminish. But the good news is that is does happen eventually. The pain subsides and the memories become warmer, richer and not something to avoid.

There has to be some relief for your mind and body. You can't sustain such intense pain and heartache. This respite comes in the form of laughter. I know you can't imagine laughing about anything again. You will have great difficulty avoiding it. Please embrace these releases from pain even if it is short lived. Force yourself to look for laughter and joy in your life. Rent your favorite comedy or call the friend who always makes you laugh. In reality, there is not a lot separating a good laugh from a good cry!

I am sure that your loved one would want you to go on with laughter and joy in your life. This doesn't mean that you're being disrespectful of their memory. Laughter in your life is the best thing you can do for yourself whenever you get the chance. Having gone through this terrible time you may find laughter in unexpected places.

Whatever you do, please take care of yourself at this most difficult time in your life.

CHAPTER EIGHT

FINAL THOUGHTS

Themes and issues raised are a result of my experience and many years of thinking about the grieving process. I hope they have been clear to you. Let me summarize what I feel are the main issues.

Our culture doesn't currently value or respect this tremendously emotional and life-altering event. The atmosphere is uncomfortable to most, during the funeral and after. Fear and helplessness are powerful feelings we deal with when confronted with someone grieving. This is especially true if we haven't yet had this experience. We face the bereaved everywhere we go. We can learn how to deal with grief in a different way.

Baby boomers are a generation with potential to make changes. Overwhelming numbers will soon be thrust into the emotional upheaval of grief. They can become an example for future generations. There is an opportunity to make a difference and to teach others who haven't yet faced this life event.

Sharing our experiences and feelings will help others support us and learn from our gained knowledge. With each shared experience, there will be a small ripple of change passed on from one to another. As these changes we have created grow our generation will be better equipped to face this tidal wave of grief.

Participation in ceremonies and rituals can help us in the grieving process. Honoring our loved one is a gratifying accomplishment. Personal touches can be woven into the funeral to make the ceremony more meaningful for all that attend. Symbols and other rituals are used to say goodbye in a meaningful way.

Taking time now to find out the wishes of those you love is highly recommended. It is not an easy subject to discuss but it will be comforting in the future to know you are honoring their memory. Information about funeral arrangements, burial preferences and gravesites gives you direction when the time comes.

Grief itself is the most important part of the book. This event cannot be experienced without pain. Trying to mask the pain will only delay the inevitable. You have to feel the pain to heal. You cannot escape. Using the resources available to manage your grief is of utmost importance.

The grief process offers an opportunity to reflect about your loved one but also your own life. The tendency is for your thoughts to turn inward about who you are and how you live. Priorities are often changed. The potential exists for relationships to become deeper and more meaningful.

The intensity of grief is a reflection of the relationship you had with the person who has died. It's hard to find the words to prepare people for this significant loss. They cannot comprehend how strong an emotional and physical response they may undergo. I describe it as an assault on the body and mind. This thunderstorm of emotions and physical symptoms seems impossible to be occurring at the same time. The force of initial grief can totally blindside you, as the intensity is not expected.

The frequency and intensity of emotions vary greatly. Many express frustration about these waves that hit without warning and explanation. You steady yourself for situations and events you expect will provoke a reaction. But these reactions happen at other times as well. The unpredictable times unnerve you the most and disturb your sense of equilibrium.

Whatever reaction you experience, there is no map to rely on for direction. There is no normal or abnormal in this process. It is individual and unique. You cannot predict your reaction to this event in your life. Each loss may produce a different reaction.

The unpredictability of reactions to grief can be disconcerting for others and us. This is why we need to trust our feelings to our friends and family.

Grief can produce many positive effects on our life. How we live will honor our loved ones who had a tremendous and powerful impact on our life.

Baby boomers have the communication tools and soon the unfortunate experience with grief to take those experiences and make even more positive changes to the world. I suspect that changing the way we handle grief will be yet another significant contribution!